BLINDSIGHT

GREG HEWETT

COFFEE HOUSE PRESS
MINNEAPOLIS
2016

Cover typeface is Aero by Chester Jenkins and Jeremy Mickel,
published by the Brooklyn-based Village type foundry.

Coffee House Press books are available to the trade through our primary distributor, Consortium Book Sales & Distribution, cbsd.com or (800) 283-3572. For personal orders, catalogs, or other information, write to info@coffeehousepress.org.

Coffee House Press is a nonprofit literary publishing house. Support from private foundations, corporate giving programs, government programs, and generous individuals helps make the publication of our books possible. We gratefully acknowledge their support in detail in the back of this book.

Library of Congress Cataloging-in-Publication Data

Names: Hewett, Greg, author.
Title: Blindsight / Greg Hewett.
Description: Minneapolis : Coffee House Press, 2016.
Identifiers: LCCN 2016006319 | ISBN 9781566894487 (softcover)
Subjects: | BISAC: POETRY / American / General.
Classification: LCC PS3558.E826 A6 2016 | DDC 811/.54—dc23
LC record available at http://lccn.loc.gov/2016006319

Printed in the United States of America
23 22 21 20 19 18 17 16   1 2 3 4 5 6 7 8

Acknowledgments

Some of the poems in this collection have appeared in the following publications: *Black Renaissance/Renaissance Noire, Boston Review, Catamaran,* the *Cincinnati Review, Denver Quarterly, Disquieting Muses Quarterly, Hanging Loose, Litscapes: Collected US Writings 2015, PRØOF,* and *Revolver.*

Continued gratitude to my comrades in verse, Ted Mathys and Chris Martin, for their friendship and guidance on matters poetic.

And to Chris Fischbach, publisher extraordinaire, who has stood by my work all these years, and to Erika Stevens, my astute new editor.

Thanks to my students Muira McCammon, Julia Bakker-Arkema, and Eli Sorich for their valuable insights.

And to my writing group: Jim Cihlar, Bill Reichard, and Christopher Tradowsky.

Special thanks to Jessica Leiman, my detail-oriented friend.

Continued amazement for having Tony Hainault in my life, and for Charlotte Irene, who has sweetened it these past six years.

This book is dedicated to Allan Kornblum (1949–2014), who first brought me into the wonderful artistic home that is Coffee House Press.

*Philosophy is written in that great book which ever lies before our eyes—
I mean the universe—but we cannot understand it if we do not first learn
the language and grasp the symbols, in which it is written. This book is
written in the mathematical language . . . without whose help it is impos-
sible to comprehend a single word of it; without which one wanders in vain
through a dark labyrinth.* —Galileo

Contents

BLINDSIGHT

Approaching Blindness

When I go out, I wear black
glasses to protect my eyes.
I walk a shadowed valley.

Inside, I wear a white shirt
to let the world outside
reflect upon the pages.

All that I cannot see, all
that I have never written,
illuminated figures.

Take blindness as metaphor,
you say, but I say
take metaphor as blindness:
deforming life to get at
the idea behind life
tires me. For too long
I have been looking

into nothing and
seen nothing
more than words.

I. Number Blind

Skyglow

When it's clear, I miss the stars.
Since their exile from the sky
I have navigated o.k. Thank heavens

for GPS, and when I get nostalgic
I still have deep space
as my screensaver.

The dark has left us too. In another time
we might have met by the river under a river

of stars.
For now

we spin filaments of light into profiles,
drawing each other
through something resembling time and space and dark.
Let's call this something something vague and mythic
as *the ether.* Let's say we're *ethereal.*

Whoever you are now texting me, when you open
the actual door I might not mistake you
for all that you've uploaded.

The TV, flickering violet behind you, is aura enough.
Glow-in-the-dark stars pasted to the bedroom ceiling are a big plus.
No matter. The whole universe is made up
of just 2% visible matter, and I am
looking for something beyond the naked eye.

Seven Fish, Three Trees, Two Men

Maybe numbers are invisible, but look
over there, seven

fish swim in the uncountable water, watched
by one man seated alone in the shade of three trees,
though none the same—oak, ash, beech.
We sense numbers in our breath,
in a line of poetry, a measure of music
running through our heads.
The truth of, say, zero, negative two, or
algebra is outside of us and all of nature,
yet somehow the absence of the man who used to come
with him is more present than the school of fish
he is watching, and the vision of the two of them,
the one gutting and filleting iridescent trout,
and then wiping his hands and the reddened blade
on his dungarees, while the other works on
a crossword puzzle,
dwells solidly in the negative space of the trees.
If he could compose the right words in a line,
or come up with an elegant equation, he's sure
he would have him back. But numbers and death are

different undercurrents of this world filled with trees,
fish, people, and so many water and so much words.

One Is the Loneliest Number That You'll Ever Do

At nineteen you rode the schizoid void like a big wave, from swell to break.
The whole universe unfurling before you was pure
numbers slamming like tweaked-out punks in the pit,
a blizzard coming at you in the headlights on an empty highway,
a coral reef forming in accelerated motion, a cloud of starlings.
Union. Division.
The suspicious equilibrium between the two.

Numbers offered omniscience,
oblique forgiveness, blindness.

They were escape from the self
and the story trailing after the self, like it was someone else's.

Five Moments of Clarity

1.

Through this glass yellowed by time,
alive with waves and bubbles,
I can see three centuries
of seeing. I see
the lost thoughts
of the mathematician who looked out from
these chambers. Numbers
materialize in the formal courtyard.
They appear fleeting,
but they are not illusions
so much as they are representations of
longing for something beyond
our human vision.
They arise from the patterns
of cobblestone, from the arc
of the fountain's jet,
from the dim portal.
The glass flows down, slow as years,
washing me into its depths.

2.

Through a cornea given
by a young girl killed
in a blizzard crash,
I could, for one clear moment
when the bandages came off,
see her seven years
of seeing, could see
what I believed was
innocence and was again
innocent in her
vision.

3.

Through the radio,
I could see the face
of the speaker's friend
torn off by shrapnel,
and him collecting
among the ruins
of the room they shared
the eyes, color gone,
and asking,
Can you now see me?
Like you, I will sell my books
for guns. I am done
with words.

4.

Through a dead language,
I can see cypress
trees lining a road,
clouds high overhead.
The landscape inspires
virtue. I breathe in
the words, every detail
articulated,
clear, as if painted
in enamel, syntax hard
and ancient as truth.

5.

Through the celestial accident that is
moonlight, I can see
toward the edge of dream.
We know it's all just electrochemical
traces, but that won't stop us.
At night we go to the top
of the highest parking ramp in this lost town
to unknow the world below,
to unexplain our desire
for something that is
hidden by daylight,
that is precisely nothing
of our own making.
We'll take this secondhand light
as our guide, this tagged structure
as our observatory
onto the invisible.

Blindsight

Never considering how his light is spent,
the mountaineer tastes the height and sheer of cliff.
He summits, triumphant. The vista resounds.
Once a blind poet saw war clear in stanzas,
weaving and unweaving heroes and horrors.
No camouflage can hide us from his vision.
Light denied, the physicist could see clearly
the structure of atoms, the complete absence
of empty space. How full the world looks beyond
the flickering tyranny of the visual.
When light lapses from my rooms I find myself
virtually lost. In blindness deep and far,
vision grows visible and the dark world wide.

The Melancholy of Primes

Like prime numbers we are made
essentially from nothing
                                but ourselves.

Sui generis? Parthenogenesis?
Narcissism? Regardless,

something cold,
                        something classical,
                        a complex from the get-go.

After 2 and 3 depart
like a train parting

                        lovers in classic
                        Hollywood fashion,

even so-called twins
like 5 and 7, 11 and 13
                        are separated at birth.

They become rarer
and rarer the farther out
                        they travel

toward infinity, floating
                        like orphaned children . . .
                        10,420,997, 10,420,999 . . .

I'm writing these lines as if
primes could really be

metaphors for existence,
as if in such loneliness
                        we discover our longing

and our attachments could be
explained by the right theorem,

                    proven in this world or not.

Finding My Rhythm

Out of step I wander off
the dance floor, out the club door,

out along lines of poetry familiar
now broken, out to the un–

spoken future pulsing under a full moon
rising, out
to right the rhythm,

write a dance
along lines hidden, out to count beats indi-
visible in Saturn's thirty-one rings revolving invisibly.

The old rhythm is changing
syllable by syllable,
step by step.

It's primal, it's primary,
it vibrates through the twenty-
nine bones of the skull,

through the twenty-nine bones that comprise the spine,
through every pair of twenty-three chromosomes
that write the tome of being,
that beyond all reckoning
hold together this

less-than–heavenly body as it orbits
outward, toward the dark
woods, with no body in mind.

Prime numbers appear
in sudden constellations
of fireflies blinking at the edge of the parking lot.

You hear them in the raucous chorus of seventeen-
year locusts penetrating deep waves of bass escaped
into this truer night life.

Seen or unseen, they are there,
uncountable, unpredictable as weeds,
precise as a regiment,
progressing
toward infinity—

and that is not just a line,
it's simply hyperbola
without plot

on any chart, a dance meant
even for the odd
likes of me

to follow solo:
the movement ametrical,
arrhythmic,

of free
and unequal duration.

As random figures appear
on the dim periphery,
I convince myself that I am that I am,
and if planets align, this time I will be
dancing as divinely as any diva,

toward something resembling eternity, under
that great disco ball of night.

II. Scenes

Zoom In

On this pixilated earth,
deep within the borders of this dominant nation,
in this state, this county, at the edge of these exurbs,
between freeway interchanges, behind a box store,
along this red stamp–sand road,
amid slag heap and ragweed,
spindly aspens and poplars,
glinting foil wrappers and superhero cups,
next to a drying puddle where a killdeer pivots,
like a giant silkworm or spawn of dragon
glowing alabaster in the morning sun,
a condom, unfurled and full,
holds dominion over this satellit world.

Because I Could Not

In elementary school I beat you up just because
the other boys tripped you when it was time to line up,
because the cafeteria lady slapped you across the face when you asked for
        a cherry in your fruit cocktail cup,
because I put you in the ring of cedars that was my castle but you just
        stepped right through, leaving me there sullen as a rock,
because I could not love, because I could not know I would need to ask
        you now, wherever you may be, *Please do not forgive me.*

Prime Time

TV sets flickered on as the sun went off the air.
I was the moody boy everyone wanted
me to be, circling the cul-de-sac like a goldfish.

Through picture windows I'd watch
all the families watching handsome bachelors
raising kids in swank penthouses and mansions.

Certain nights I'd orbit out and find myself
in deserted parking lots,
facing men definitely not for prime time.

My disciplined parents would be nodding off
to "The Star-Spangled Banner" when I came home.

Where've you been? they'd ask by rote.
Shooting hoops, I'd answer with a sitcom grin.

Senior Pic, '76

It's what you'd expect:
a pair of stoned eyes behind
aviator frames, mutton
chops down the jawline,
hair flipped up like wings,
wide lapels, velvet bow tie,
background of fake sky.
We're all retro once
or twice in our lives.
They airbrushed acne
from the cheeks and lust
right out of the eyes,
or they definitely tried.

Like small moons of quartz
at the bottom of a well,
images remain glowing:
catalog models in white
T-shirts tucked into white briefs,
the untamed body of each
teammate in the gang shower,
the hippies spied on
skinny-dipping down
at the falls, a play
replayed scene-by-scene,
in which a buck-naked boy
blinds horses with a hoof pick.

All of that desire
in those wasted eyes,
all of that desire wasted.

Yearbook

The blank next to me—
no picture available—
that long-forgotten shadow,
that fag, that sissy, that fem,
that boy we bullied,
dropped out and drifted
to the city long before
graduation. I am not
afraid of him now.
I have mounted him
in a frame hinged to my own,
a kind of double portrait.
You'd almost think we were twins.

Blindsided

Circumstance sits across the table from me
like a doctor or a lawyer, in a room too clean,
breaking news too quietly.

Fortune arrives, a demon demolition
derby king, flipping a doughnut on my life.
We narrowly escape the crash of rivals, the fiery explosion.

But there is always the one
you don't see, the one
prying his front-end loose, reversing out of the pyre,
accelerating with a statistician's vengeance
toward the driver's side, the crowd going wild.

The Passion of Andrew Grande

1. *Oceanside Motel*

You know you're deep into porn
when randomly you turn on

the TV in a motel
to catch the local

weather and it's clear you know
the guy on the news,

described as a would-be gay
porn-star, in what they say is

a *domestic* [sic] in
a parking lot not unlike
the one outside your locked door.

2. *The Weather*

Begin with the wind,
the rain,
the dust

(there is dust
even here
in wet ocean wind),

on my face
more real
than Weather

Channel visuals
and the news
it's the end

of the hurricane.
Like his story, not major.

But words cannot make
wind more real,
rain more real,

dust more real,
his body more real.

3. *Andrew Grande / Dustin*

Did his mother know
that *Andrew* means *man*,
like *andro*,
that she had named him
something glorious
(and also something porny),
Great Man?

Did he know his nom de guerre
means the same? *Dustin.*

Did he know he was
a great man
as he roamed

hot Alabama
nights looking
for the best way out?

Slurpies and pussy and weed—
the big three when you're chillin'
and ridin' around.

In Alabama
they loved him, a girl or two.

In Alabama
did they know
he was a great man?

4. *Ride-Along*

It's not clear whether he shoves
the woman or not,

but he is slamming
his fist on the hood

of the SUV
she enters as the police

arrive on the scene.
It's also not clear

how this footage came to be,
until the announcer says
their crew just happened
to be on a ride-along.
A ride-along just happens?

5. *White Caucasian Male [sic]*

I am doing lines of you
Dustin,

dust of my dust, self
of my self,

a white Caucasian [sic]
male, unarmed,

self-described *white boy, white trash,*
like me. I

don't want to lose you
to this world

of news, just one more
video upload.

I want to take you
to my grandmother's
trailer in the woods,
where she'd hobble out
on one leg to examine
you with her one eye
and heal you.

6. *A Dumb Thing to Do*

What we see doesn't matter.
We're told he resists arrest.

He pulls something from his jeans
and swallows it. We are told

it's marijuana in a
plastic bag. Probably true.
A dumb thing to do.

7. *Gay4Pay*

Amateur and *straight* have lost meaning in this
world; those words
a big draw, hence sites like *Broke Straight Boys,* where Dustin ruled

with his declaration of poverty and heterosexuality:
No dude's ever gonna fuck me unless there's a deed to a big house involved.

8. *Tase Him*

The police don't seem to see or seem to know
what to do, so they tase him.
At first he constricts and writhes, but then he is just so

earnest—like an allegorical figure
of Earnestness—and then desperate, exasperated.

Finally, on his knees, he's pleading so quietly,
like the perfect supplicant.

9. *Loser*

He'd be laughing his ass off
watching this, a costar says,
if it wasn't him.

10. *Pantomime*

On the 32-inch screen
the great man
pantomimes

dying.
Only it is real.
He's already dead
and I
have touched his body

in the way that porn tricks us,
firing off mirror neurons
throughout our bodies.

Just once did he kiss
a man—sweet Danny—
and it seemed so real.

But that certain look
of death can't be faked,
though you can't *see* death.

11. *Tricks*

Once he told me to rim him,
another model says, *and then farted in my face.*
He hated
anyone who fell
for his tricks.
But then he would fall asleep
like a baby, with his head on my belly.

12. *Rude and Mean*

On the *Broke Straight Boys* website
after his death, it says: *He got rude and mean.*
Besides, he was getting bald and fat, and his cum shots
were never that great.
Thank God for him he had a sugar daddy.

13. *Liable*

Even when his body went
limp, the police could still not figure out what
was going on, and the news
crew, who did see, did nothing.
He was twenty-three.

14. *The Crux of Fiction*

The most real he ever seemed
was when it was fictional,

at least a greater fiction
than when all the boys supposedly just came

off the street
and plunked their junk down
on the blue futon

to perform their amateur
straight-boy act.

On a related website
the guys are supposed to be

college athletes going in
for their physicals

(implausibly together).
Of course they then get it on

with each other or the doc,
sometimes a male nurse.

Andrew couldn't afford to go
to the doctor or college,

but plays the part well.
He'd worked with Danny before,

but for some reason
(there isn't much of a script)

on the cold exam table
they start kissing as though starved

for life, and it is impossible to say
whether it is performance.

There's no proof,
but a poem

he wrote for his church
bulletin is evidence

of passion for a beloved
who in death becomes

ungendered and remembered
with tenderness—this surely

the way he would want to be
remembered himself:

A Broken Heart,
Is hard to repair
It takes some Love
And people who care
Missing the person,
Who I Loved so dear,

Made me shed,
Some crippling tears,
Praying I had
Just one more day,
Wanting to hug them,
And so much to say,
Sometimes forgetting,
That they are no longer around,
And then suddenly think,
And know whom they've found,
Their body may,
Be in a grave,
But before they died I saw them saved,

Then a smile spread across my face
Knowing they are in a much better place.

Andrew Grande, did you believe
in a better place?

What does it look like?
Some big house?

A gated community?
No sugar daddies allowed?

You would hate this poetry,
unrhymed, documentary,

but you would hate it much more
if I imagined

your interior
monologue or put you in

made-up scenes,
maybe not with wings

and flying through the ether,
but a god

(in the colloquial sense)
wading through the camouflage-

beauty
of an Alabama swamp.

You have been granted
an approximation of eternal life,

virtually, having sex
and dying anytime and

anyplace that's wired,
a world

without recompense,
without punishment,

though I can't resist judgment
and hereby place these stolen lines on your tongue,

as you survey the circles
within circles of porn sites in which you dwell:

. . . all of the countless many . . .
who would
have thought so many undone?

[phantom lines]

You thought you knew me because you'd seen me nut.
Seeing is not believing.

Did you ever see me with the camera off?
As I saw myself when I wasn't wasted?
Did you even know the color of my eyes?

Can you see my soul?
It's as visible as time.

III. Mind's Eye

At the Same Table

Memory tells me
I see us

      still sitting
      at that same sidewalk table,
      but do I really

have that image or
don't I

      also see
      the table and beer glasses
      and you there

from the same
point of view
as then and not see

      myself? If I were
      to call you

all these years later,
I am still sitting
at that same table

      waiting for you, although not
      as I would see it.

If you want
an image of what
you once called my soul,

      then listen
      to all that I see,
      it's right there

in my body voiced,
translated
into you.

Against Nostalgia

Not just the usual tricks of memory,
like, was your polo bright red or powder blue?
Even if words arranged themselves like pixels,
the past will never become completely clear.
Why, decades later, do you, stranger, remain
a *you* despite the mayfly status of everything
between us and not a single word ever exchanged,
while the one I lived with five years will always be *he*?
Remain you,
one-hundred-sixty-million-eight-hundred-thirty-three-thousand-five-
    hundred-and-ninety-three, and counting, mayfly life-spans ago,
because you looked at the sun and then at me and smiled
as we showered under a single broad head on a hostel roof overlooking a
    bright sea.
Even if that memory can be trusted,
smile is a word as vacant as the blue summer sky,
a word I still don't know how to fill to make the picture more than just
    soft-core.
I would like to insist it wasn't about the look or the looking,
that it was about both of us simply being there, all Zen, glazed with salt
    and sand, sunburned, standing under iron-cold water tasting of
    iron, waves flashing below,
about not knowing what your expression meant and not thinking about
    it, let alone words for it, or at least I would like to believe it was
    like that:
a world before lust: my brain squints trying not to look below your waist.
It was, I tell myself, about not thinking
that we would never be there in that moment again
and that we would in the far future be held apart by these words (you
    will never read), memory (at least mine) strained beyond sight or
    sensibility (did the freckles on your shoulders form a constellation
    of lizard or bird? and was that polo shirt you pulled over your head
    as you descended into the deep shadow of the dining hall scarlet or
    sky blue?),
and that syntax, the very structure of thought, would be taxed by long-
    ing to the point of fracture.

How Memory Kills

A random story of an ancient Greek poet comes to me just as a fighter
      jet cruises fifteen miles overhead
in this the least Greek town imaginable, at this, the least Greek bar in
      the world, if they even had bars, the Greeks that is.
The blue twilight could be Greek, without the jet of course, except the
      fact they apparently didn't see blue—the sky was bronze; honey,
      green; oxen, purple.

In any case, I'm bellied up, getting wasted on tequila, thinking of this
      poet at a symposium, which was something like a Greek gay bar
      but with more talking, philosophizing.
Most likely he was recumbent on a sofa, blitzed from imbibing that
      piney wine they call *retsina,* and offering ninety-nine words for
      love, when the pillars came tumbling down in a temblor, killing
      all his friends.
Soon he could not remember any of them and cried, *This is grief worse*
than death!

Eventually he started to recall all the architectural details of the hall:
the orders of columns and pilasters, cornice, tympanum, the frieze with
      bas-reliefs showing the gods in better times.
He then reconstructed in his mind the room with all of the furniture,
      and slowly the dead began to return, laughing and calling to each
      other across the space.

I start memorizing each mesmerizing neon beer sign, the length of the
      bar, the wood it's made from (oak), the swinging doors, ceiling
      beams, glass-block windows,
wondering if I will be the one lucky or unlucky enough to be left to re-
      member the dead if the jet falls on this place, *deus ex machina,*
      from the bronze sky.

And though no one here has yet spoken to me of the sweet, green nature
      of love,
still something like love arises bronze-bright and clear amid the purple
      terror of forgetting.

Memoir

It is and it is
not the way
we tell stories around here.

We want it just once
upon a time, yet

the man at the door
of this stanza is a ghost

of his former self
and a monster from

time to time. Something's
about to happen,

but it's difficult to tell
anything at all.

On days the fog lifts,
it isn't any clearer.

Eucalyptus pollen and
malaise drift down over all.

It's apples *or* oranges
in the wooden bowl.

Under this fine patina
we're as abstract as statues.

The air blurs
motive and gesture.
A hand raised means anything.

No journalists are camped out
to get the story

of our metaphoric crimes.
It's easy to imagine

there's no prequel or sequel
or spin-off to living so

uneventfully,
no story

arcing toward rescue,
no happy ever after,

but at least
I never promised
you Armageddon.

Nebulous Apocalypse

If there were one second left,
I'd say there is more

than love and nothing
more than love, than burying

my face in your crotch—
divine funk of marigolds!

Even in the last
millisecond I'd refuse
to terminate the story.

In the grace of you,
in a concluding embrace,

I would have us flung skyward
at the speed of light

and we would become
twin constellations,

the warrior and the pansy
or some such.

A nano-epic
or just

asterisks above
our brief existence

like so*
and so*

Resurrection Fantasy

If you were to burst out of your tomb, superhero-
style, stone slab flying away like Styrofoam,
would I be the one

tumbling backwards and down the swell of earth, afraid, awed,
or would I be folded in upon myself, asleep,
lantern glowing by my side?
Or maybe just a passerby, confused by the ways
of death? But you won't come back,
and I am safe betting that
a calcium-white angel will not descend.

Even in speculation this scene is not
polished chiaroscuro
like a Renaissance painting,
but coarse like Ben-Day dots in a comic book,
your thought a bubble,
Resurrection is, like, so overrated,
as you smirk wisely, wildly—that look I love.

Waterfall

Walking the edge of the pool,
looking for revelation
in the chaos of water.
Dawn to dusk, bass stay concealed
under oblique shelves of shale.

Behind the falling water,
nearly invisible, a luckier man
pulls out fish after fish, like a magician.

Between us, a turtle the size of a shield
cruises the eddying deep,
or maybe it's just shadow.

If I could cross the abyss
growing within me,
if I could cross this ravine,

I'd join him under the falls,
I'd enter the realm
where trophies leap and shimmer.

On a Back Road, Summer Night

Alongside the car, a white horse gallops as if it were the apocalypse.
In the halogen headlights, gravel shines as hard as marble fragments.
Under the dead weight of summer, night air collapses.

As I pull off into grass, the beast comes so sweetly,
barbed-wire scars down his muzzle, vivid in moonlight.

He tugs the aromatic offering from my fist.
Across the dark marsh, will-o'-the-wisp twinkles as if it were Christmas.

Seeing Things

Just when I think I am getting old and seeing things
through nostalgia's wicked warp,
I read that songbird numbers have plummeted
by something ridiculous
since I was a kid, and that we see fewer
than half the stars we used to.
The crazed blizzard of finches
in forsythia out my childhood window,
and the menagerie of constellations
that swallowed me and the yard
and the sky, were just as real as the last owl
rising like a pterodactyl from the oaks for good
when the new dealership illuminated our world.

Bright Spring Days

Some days we forget our loss
by recalling bright spring days
in poems we wrote as kids

and called *Bright Spring Days Part I*
and *II:* "Bright sun, come to me!"
We forget those days held night

rain dripping from eaves like gold,
lilac shadows on the lawn,
crows among the tulip beds.

We forget that light echoes
through the world obscurely
even at noonday, even

when clouds clear and we see clear
past the parking lot, farther
than the orderly border
of arborvitae, something
floating there like memory.

Witness

There's a car crash in my head
from when I was just a kid.

They told me it was TV
but that would be black and white.

They told me it was a dream
but that I wouldn't remember.

She's there, in a frosty field
fired rose by dawn,
a girl of my age,
the color of ice,
asleep in a ring of fire,

as if a father or king had laid her there
for safety or sacrifice or desire.

I stood in sunrise,
BB gun held like a lance,

her unprepared protector
from forces greater than us.

River Stone

Watching a boy skip stones across the river,
I'd like to believe his soul is smooth as river stone.

Even if souls are just so much poetry—and this,
too much poetry—it's good to think of his

as innocent, that innocence still exists
and might be compressed and held fast in the palm, or worn,
an amulet resting cool against the throat.

My Grandmother's House

I want to write about my grandmother's house, though this is not my
       grandmother's house, this house guarded by spruce, set in fields
       of flax.
She lived in a sooty apartment overlooking the shipyards, yet this old
       farmhouse is where I see her, moving on swollen legs through
       rooms big as thoughts.
There isn't even a house here anymore, just the memory of a house I used
       to pass, a milky aura against a sky convoluted and gray as a brain.
It was abandoned even then, and I'd always imagined the rooms resounding
       hollow if I walked around in them,
hollow, as if rooms would miss the lives that had been lived within their
       walls, as if hollowness made memory more profound,
as if our cramped, crammed lives were not worth remembering,
as if memory flows from the heart to the eye, not the other way around.

Indigo Bunting / *Passerina cyanea*

1. *The Bunting of Happiness*

That blue bird is not a bluebird is an indigo
bunting, my father taught me
when I was a boy.

Without the bluebird's red breast,
these winged scraps of sky
rise and fall
in patterns of disappearance, blue on blue,
like memories of him do.

Like birds, words can fly
farther than the eye:
a tale from India of an indigo tail feather dropped by an avatar.

If the feather would only lead me to a father-
figure or blue-skinned god, one beyond human

imagination or sight—in other words,
unbelievable—I could just make believe

and follow that bird up through sky upon sky,
oblivious to change in altitude or
latitude, follow
that blue bird in extremis
or maybe to nirvana.

Whichever state awaits me,
my mood doesn't turn so blue
when a great flock of indigo buntings passes through.

2. *Of Unhappiness*

Paterfamilias, you taught me the Latin
names for birds: the vulgar *blue*
bunting took on smooth, aerodynamic tones: *Passerina cyanea.*

You're history now, and now
I see flocks of migrating blue buntings as spearheads
of an ancient army, raised, militant to the sky.
When bronze corrodes to cyan it is somehow strengthened,
the way history is by memory, I suppose.
Showing not telling was cuneiform to you, so I will just say, yes,
I'm still angry with you for dying so soon.

In the fractured crucible
of language, *cyan*—
the oldest word in the world—becomes the modern
spy's *cyanide,* and I would gladly have bitten that capsule in two,
except it wouldn't have saved you,
because time and time again, death's the greatest
counterintelligence operation in the world.

A Gift for My New Daughter

When in the future I place
this amber bracelet around your wrist and clasp

the drops of sunlight
cool against your skin,

there is no intention to
enclose
like beauty, like memory, like possession,

like a father's love can seem.
It will, I promise,
open.

Look within the stones,
sweet girl:

pine pollen floating there in fiery light
can become a forest deep
and cool as ocean.

I can see your blue eyes flash
in wavelight: accept this gift as horizon.

A Gross Exaggeration

When I told my mother as she was making to-do lists about how a poet
   before he was a poet saw a girl dressed in crimson and when he
   saw her again passing along the street nine years later (this time
   dressed in the whitest of white) she turned her eyes toward him
   and God suddenly appeared in flames, thus changing the whole
   history of poetry, she said that was a gross exaggeration.

When I told my mother as she sat doing her bills about how a baker saw
   a young woman coming in to buy bread and, though he would
   never see her again, the grace of her fingers dropping coins into
   his floury palm and then drawing the crisp warm loaf to her
   breast was so profound that he started speaking poetry (though
   he knew none at all before then) and from that moment on wrote
   poems about her, neglecting his business and wasting away in
   poverty, she said he needed to have his head examined.

When I told my mother as she worked on sudoku puzzles about how her
   own son, while stopping for gas, watched a guy (lean as a wolf and
   in scarlet leathers) rise up in the saddle of his snowmobile as he
   tore at warp speed out of the evergreens and across the snowy field
   and continued watching as he pulled up to the pump and raised his
   visor, revealing a face that could launch an epic that might take ten
   years of her son's life, she said that's great, just great.

Nowhere, Everywhere

Walking along the road, I pick up a stone
to throw to about nowhere.
A boyhood habit, but this one time I don't.
This ordinary fact of geology remains
in my hand and I am lost
in its rough geography,
its steep ridges and plateaus,
its valleys and depressions.
If I could draw this world
in pen and ink, just as intricate as it exists—
draw it big as a mural—
will I at last discover
in the labyrinth
of patient labor
that there's no greater vision
than in finally seeing
details reigning everywhere?

The Village

There's a photo of a girl
and she's laughing light.

She sits in a worn rowboat
between two women at oars

just three days before it all
was gone, when her world was still

rowing boats and herding geese
and skipping through the village

on her way to school, to church,
as the exhibit teaches.

After killing the people,
after erasing the town,
like it was a picture drawn,

the soldiers buried the lake
as if they were blinding God.
The geese flew away.

One year, the lake made it back,
and again reflected sky.

In memory, pain returns,
domesticated, like geese,

like geese in a row sailing
shore to shore

under the old sun,
below the new museum,

through these words
insignificant

as the dog that barks
in metallic morning light
from *the replacement village,*
as the guide calls it,
built right across the valley.

The Artist

An artist studies a young boy drawing in a field,
his lambs more real than those frisking in front of them.

He asks if the boy can draw
a circle, and he does one perfect, freehand.

He asks him to paint the color of heaven,
and the saints appear.

He calls the boy an artist,
and the boy will spend his life

in search of the lambs
and the circle he has drawn,
at last building a tower
of cloud-like marble to reach
a heaven he still can't see.

IV. P.O.V.

The Drowning

It comes like a thought,
the figure rising to the lake's calm surface
indistinct as an angel.

The public gathers onshore
reflecting

on what has transpired, on what is transcending.
Either you recognize yourself or you don't.

There's no way to know
a life by examining
its features; the facts
skip like stones across
the surface, then sink.

They'll do the ID,
though that's not the idea
of someone, the idea

one has of one's self
beyond all identity,

one's self to oneself, that place
where clarity disappears.

Instructions for Forgetting

There is a word I can't remember for forgetting
who I am, for erasing

all those guideposts that every moment bring us
back to the garage of who we think we are,

the inner
monologue building up slowly, discreetly, like carbon monoxide.
Not *amnesia*. It's more intentional than that.

Every brain ought to
come with special emergency instructions:

buy a last-minute ticket to anyplace
you've never heard of;

discard all electronic devices, credit cards;
buy a new wardrobe;

on arrival, be sure the city reads like
a journal unlike your own;

excise your name and picture from your passport
and leave it on a park bench;

destroy photos; remember,
landscape is harder to forget than people;
now find a hotel, someplace

anonymous (apartments
become us too easily);

avoid grand boulevards with memorials
to the knowns or the unknowns;

don't learn the local language;
visit museums with collections that interest you

not in the least (farm implements, ceramic
tile ovens, a whole mansion of op art);

on the outskirts, visit battlefields of wars
that never became history; see ruins;

wander train stations;
don't buy a ticket;
eat at lunch counters;

frequent neighborhoods
where those as foreign as you

have begun to forget where
they came from, what they came for.

Self-Portrait as Greek Hero

The bronze helmet fits so I wear it, liking its shiny defiance.
A visor obscures the fear encamped in my features.

An army of bright chariots, photons pour into my eyes and die,
lending epic valor and violence to my well-fortified glare.

Visitors to the exhibit almost believe I'm a demigod,
but then detect the wristwatch I forgot to take off.
Illusion in ruins, the weapons of loneliness now glint all around me.

Self-Portrait as Heartbroken Prom Queen, circa 1967

Even for old guys like me, the look's the easy part:
prosthetics, wig, vintage clothes, an hour with Photoshop.
The mussed beehive does the trick.

It's the once-upon-a-time-
I-was-my-daddy's-princess-but-now-nothing-matters
feeling that's tough to master:

I fall onto a retro champagne-satin bedspread,
eyes wide-open like a girl
murdered in the woods at night, imagining

the harvest-gold rotary phone won't ring no matter how much I swear
        to God
I will never ever act like such a bitch again.
TV-light reflecting off my unwashed face says that vocab word *abjection*
        like nothing else.

In the deep-focus background there's a picture of me and him at winter
        prom
—him an absence in black—me a swirl of white,
a regular snow queen, holding red roses.

At a distance it looks like I've been slashed wide open,
but really I'm so happy as they hand me my crown.
It's tough work being me, she and I decide with a sigh and a yawn.

Whether it is drama or trauma is hard
for anyone to know. We search the mirror
as we're falling asleep, dreaming of future losses.
By the time I wake up I am a glittering mess.
Wig fallen off, rhinestones biting into my bald crown, and a suspicion
        that the pumps have begun to fit a little too well.

Goat in the Thicket

Capricious wish, I know, but
a goat's-eye view of the world
would double my field

of vision—a pan-
orama, or nearly so:
340 degrees.

Rectilinear pupils,
horizontally aligned,
might freak people out,

but out of those wide corners
I could finally see God
sneaking up from behind or

know it is a breeze or man
in the deep thicket, swishing
across my haunches instead.

I'd be under the aegis
of no one but me,

though there's danger I'd forget
a blind spot exists at all.

Vulnerable to every kind
of scapegoating, with no cab
to hail for escape,

I'd wind up singing
a goatsong so true,
tragedy at its purest.

I am by nature
a comedian, though, so

I'd wish for chameleon eyes,
but they're not in the Bible.

Motel

In the desert of every heart there's a motel
where you leave the numbered door open at night
to allow the random sphinx moth or stranger
to float in with blue light from the swimming pool,
like spirits, if spirits had flesh and were still spirits.
One, with a body perfect
as a busted–up cowboy

glued back together again,
enters to tell you the story of your life
like it was his very own.
Though the story is all wrong
in every detail, he's right
about the solitary nature of life:
Every damn one of us comes from a place far away

as nowhere, traveling to each new no–place
to be missed, an ongoing kind of death wish.
And as much as you want him
to turn you into a country song, he won't
call this motel love, won't call it loneliness.

The Prodigal Dad

Like the sacrificial bull he always thought he was,
he returned garlanded heavily with opiates,
no less strung out than the day he headed off.

No bunting, no festoons, no celebration ensued.
One of the kids popped a wheelie on the ATV.
They hardly knew him, except for the brooding.

Some say he saw his grown son standing there in the sun
as the living word, as the shining sword that would one day slaughter him,
and grew so afraid he took a hoe used for snakes and struck the boy down.

Some say the son walks, a phantom among us;
others say a stranger flew out from the gas station across the road,
that he hid him for three days and nights in the dusty crack of river,
that they lived on dew gathered from cactus leaves,
that he healed the fatal wound at his temple,

that they found sanctuary on the freeway,
that it was a miracle, and the father lived on,
trapped in this parable, like an insect in amber.

Anonymize Now

We want to know you
and not get to know
you at all.

We've got your number
encrypted

and you're not even
dead yet.
For your protection

we're providing you
with a mathematical

blindfold,
so only you cannot see
how much

it's going to hurt
when we begin to strip you

of identity.
There's really nothing

wrong, just so long as
you're doing nothing
wrong, and certainly

we all know
when that's happening.
In the end

it's practically
like meeting strangers
back in the day when

there were still strangers,
those lonely people
before we all got social.

Hitchhiker

I dream cars, never
the driver—his face, his hands,
his crotch—the things a passenger might notice.

I'm always on the shoulder,
vision platonic.
No shadows hold the bodies

to the earth. They float
like their chassis were bird bone.
Clear as mirages, they speed

slowly toward me, daring me
to make them stop, to
court danger.

They dare me to imagine
just how ideal they will be,
but I never do.

And yet, true to form,
the one that picks me up comes

at the hour least obscure—
the sun straight up—when I am shadowless, too.

Your Totem Takes On the World

Sometimes you wake up so wrong,
   like maybe you're on the wrong
      channel and if you go back
   to sleep you'll have the good luck
to wake up as a berserk
   wolf–bear or bear–wolf, something
      all mythy, greasy, and fierce.
   A most excellent program,
in which you get to attack
   the world shaped like a hunk
      torn from a Baroque palace,
   a trophy-torsoed warrior,
something from a museum.
   It's smackdown time. You're ready.
      You decide you like living
   allegory—it's so clear.
He's hard and shiny, and hard
   to hold on to, like silver
      and marble impossibly,
   unnaturally alloyed.
You plaster the pompous gloss
   with salmon guts and ripened
      muskrat entrails and berries,
   and wrap yourself tight around
anaconda-style, squeezing
   until the world cries *Uncle!*
      You drag said world to a place
   obscured by echoes and firs,
a place far off-camera,
   where waking and sleep are one.
      This, at last, is victory.

The Eighth Deadly Sin

It's not any ordinary laziness.
Not sadness alone.

You sit on the roof in rain,
watching leaves spiral

into the rusted gutters,
to collect and dam

around the oily remains
of an oriole.

When the house collapses, you'll hardly notice.
You'll close the curtains.

You'll be thinking of a god,
maybe wondering why you
run away as fast as you approach even the most

believable one,
the one without beard or voice,
space or time, the one

who comes on
like a concussion.

Streets, cities, even countries,
you've seen afflicted by this forgotten sin.

Buildings begun, left unfinished. Roads vanished.
The sky suddenly too far.

It is less like sloth
than a slow leaching of spirit. It takes years

before we understand it
has gone way too far,

before we can feel the hurt,
before we notice
the sun's begun to blacken.

The Grand Tour

The world is so picturesque, why not hang it above the mantel?
Mounted there, it's infinitely easier to see,
no vista obscured, only a lonely cloud or two.
Each peak displays nimble climbers harnessed fast
to our enlightened vision. To look inward—

to dwell in the mind's own grotto—is grotesque.
Things there, only imagined:
thundering blindness so complete we beg for lightning.

If we were to hide an infrared camera inside
of that convoluted crypt,
our selves would horrify ourselves—we'd evacuate.

Camp X-Ray

Exclusive beachfront property, location undisclosed. Very VIP.
Don't worry about the paperwork, we've got our attorneys on it.
Invisible fences for an unobstructed view.
The military is here to entertain you. They are a riot.
What you have done or not done doesn't much matter. It's the thought
       that counts.
Light provided 24-7 to assist you
in flooding every last dark corner of your dark heart.
We'll open your mind, we'll make it visible.
Water helps with transparency, too. It's the latest in rack and screw,
so retro it's new.
In short, we'll see right through you.

The Magic Lantern

With no definite purpose in mind I go online and find magic
lantern images of swimmers I once saw

as a kid on one of those museum trips.
They looked like men to me then,

though the placard called them *youths,*
said they were *bathing.*
Their very innocence once

lacking resolution has been carefully restored,
appearing highly defined, like bas-relief: naked

as fish, they horse around, dive like otters, shattering
pattern after pattern of sun on water.

At the edge of the surrounding woods, obviously
invisible to us, a man, most probably clothed,
framed them

with his apparatus invented specifically
for the scientific study of motion.

Maybe he had shown the boys
a horse cantering, a deer bounding, a dove flying,

all there in the dark cave of his studio.
They too could become creatures

of a modern god in love
with light and motion.

Maybe he told them this. Maybe he told them
everything is pure

science—love, beauty,
camaraderie—everything.

Maybe he really believed in this flickering world,
maybe the boys believed his every word,
leaving me there, stranded and alone, on the far shore.

Boy Riding a Snow Shovel

In the movie everyone's seen and I've seen
only in fragments scattered
over dozens of Christmases and never the end,
the hero, when still a boy—
brightly dark in black-and-white—

in one lightning motion picks up a shovel,
jumps down on the wide blade, handle thrust between his legs,
and flies down a hill outside a town that is
perfect—and the hill, too—there,
constructed on a soundstage, with artificial snow.
Yet somehow the bliss, the joy, the glee—all words
now nearly extinct—

exist within him,
in his swift descent,
and they're real as gravity.

Gravity too takes
another boy down the hill,
but farther—too far—
out onto a fake river,
and he falls through the fake ice
into real water (piped in
and not very cold). The boy
who is the hero dives in
after him, and though
the danger seems less
than bliss, joy, glee—less believable—it does

somehow seem crucial,
like it is telling us we can never know
danger outside what is real.

Foreign Film in Fog

No desire in sight,
you take a streetcar to the end, to the beach.
The ocean is a TV with the picture turned off.
There's nothing to see but a neon marquee pulsing through the curtain
    of air.
You enter and find yourself in a long foreign biopic about a brilliant
        mathematician who lived a century ago and had bad luck in love
        and a hill on the dark side of the moon named after her.
And when you go out into the world again,
clarity greets you, like a well–rehearsed shark.

Features

1. *The Director's Cut*

You automatically start running a stranger's life just like time–
lapse photography in reverse—a flower in full bloom furling up
petals, curling back down into the dark earth, into its cozy seed:

from his last swallow of beer
flowing up through his muscled,
razor–burned throat, chug by chug,
back up into the longneck;
to the desperate horniness
that lasted his first necktied week in a cubicle
after college, maybe a decade ago;

to a paneled family room with his high–school buddy,
their skinny hips lifting from beanbag chairs in unison to the beat
of their favorite band;

to a cool ravine where he catches crayfish
and recognizes himself for the first time
as someone else on the bright, rippled surface;

all the way back to that microcosmic splash
in his mother's womb, that disappears like a specter
back into his father's shaft before rushing
up the labyrinth of the vas deferens
to once again come to rest in the testes.

Just as you start projecting the two of you as this
double feature twisted like a double helix, with the one movie playing
backward, the other forward, simultaneously,

you realize your direction is all wrong.
There's no documentary
evidence to speak of (in fact, he hasn't spoken a single word)
so you pull the plug on this new project, postponing
the big premiere of desire.

2. *The Best Porn*

The best porn is lying back
on destroyed sheets just watching
the one who occupied your bed last night coming out of the shower.

It gets a little slapstick because you forgot to lay out towels
and he probably thinks you're asleep and is too polite to wake you,
so tiptoes from room to room, gathering up his clothes, twisting and
jerking like a comic genius on a tightrope, as he tries not to drip
all over your hardwood floors.

Still, bending over for boxers, he is sexy only because he is not
trying too hard, or really trying at all, like in romantic comedies (at least
the more memorable ones,
in which the guy's a little goofy), especially
when he looks over to your half-closed eyes, maybe more
nervous than longing, maybe
indifferent or regretting he ever came,
or just perplexed as to whether you're asleep or not.

In the end it seems more documentary,
when he nods and shrugs as he unbolts the door, leaving
a chain of sad little lakes that you trace with your toe,

except the light's like the lighting in a tearjerker,
where sunbeams glitter with dust,
or the end of a disaster flick, the hero mourning among the ruins.

V. Spectacle

Eyewitness

Most nights I see things. Clockless, time assembles
orderly as a flood, each moment fluid
as dream, each action a rock in the torrent.
From what wrecked dimension did these unpinioned
angels appear outside my window tonight,
flying over freeway hazard, zigzagging
around cars? When sirens washed the air ruby,
they became just boys. They dove into the dark.
I heard no gunfire, saw only shooting stars.
At last the blue hour came in like the tide,
the world without surveillance; silent, at rest.

That Opal Feeling

Sometimes it arrives and is
out of place as opera on
the soundtrack of a thriller

      you're not really following.
      It is not the specifics—
      soprano? Italian?—or even music.

         Like opal, is all
         you can think
         (the word dull, humble,
         not fired with charisma like *sapphire, diamond*)
         and don't stay for the credits,

            don't remember the movie,
            don't want the music
            to go on inside your head.

      Opal, made of light
      and water as much as stone.
      Solid illusion,
      they break easily,
      should not be given,
      should stay hidden in
      boxes, velvet-lined.

It is something like drowning
in a deep, clear lake,
to be
imprisoned inside
a giant opal,
and you find yourself dying
as you try to breathe
one single fragment
resembling something

            so completely lost
            to this world as *beauty*.

Like this, but not exactly:
from below you're staring up
as sun breaks
into a million prisms
falling down all around you.

A Dove Dives into Its Nest

If I were that dove, I'd live in your hedge, too.
Without innuendo. I've never met you.
Or even seen you. Though passing as I do

every day. Your façade is invisible.
If behind that green a house exists at all.
Or yard. Or garden. It may all just be wall.

Labyrinth to wander. Made of evergreen.
Privet, pine, cypress, cedar, yew. Every green.
Labyrinth to wonder. Made of every dream.

If I could find just one explicit portal,
I wouldn't desire a single other world.

Seen or unseen. My open wings would reveal
my motives for you who will only conceal.

Parable of the Spider

A translucent spider moves
on articulate legs over the expanse of gray
wood paneling, less like an arachnid than a man

who has lost his way
between truth and lust.

He skitters without progress
toward no goal except his own

survival by way of thread
explained into web as complicated as
it is tenuous—a stretch.

A feat of vanity, yes,
yet the tensile arrangement
witnessed here, engineered to defy belief—

vibrating in the breeze, glittering in scraps of sun—
is well deserving
of praise without spin

from the one who lies
on the sofa ignorant of the dangers
spiders face; on the ceiling, a lizard flicks its tail.

The Dinner Party

If you will excuse me please,
the molecules were delish—
smoke under glass, sea-foam à la mode, artichoke air—
and the conversation most
civilized, convivial as yoga class.
But I must confess I would prefer to slip
under the teak tabletop
with my host and pray
for something a little more transubstantial,
a private carnival amid the forest of legs,
a time for meat and dirty
talk, inter-courses, of course.
So I bid adieu to the invisible
fabulousness of your modernist glass box
because I'm afraid
I cannot see the forest
for the glass, and like a prince enamored of
the darkest regions, only
there will I find rest.

Echo

When I close my eyes
everything is clear.

The right words will come.
I will write them down.

But when I open my eyes,
everything becomes echo
of words within words.

Rosewind

The rose is victim
of the visible

        even here
        past the last

        garden of the last
        suburb,
        blooming

        so solitary
        in a field.

Petals carry the burden
of all that color.

Light is
heavier than so
much else.

The rose is victim
of vision,

        unfolding untold
        tons of poetry.

Love is
heavier than so
much else.

Wind tilts the blossom
like a truck,

        spilling its cargo
        over everything.

In this
rosewind

      what can't be seen shows
      everywhere,

      like arrows
      on a weather map,

      like the whole prehistory
      of the visible

      revealed
      layer by layer,

      the bones of vision
      everywhere.

Notes

The structure of this collection, the form of the poems in it, and
the rhythm of each line derive from the music and writings of Olivier
Messiaen, in particular his use of prime numbers in composing music.

p. vii The Galileo epigraph is from *The Assayer* (1623), as translated
by Thomas Salusbury, as quoted in *The Metaphysical Foundations of
Modern Science* by Edwin Arthur Burtt, p. 64 (New York: Harcourt,
Brace, 1925).

p. 7 The title of this poem is the first line of the song "One" by Harry
Nilsson.

p. 10 Some of the language in this section of the poem comes from one
of Kelly McEvers's interview subjects in a story she did on the Palestinian
conflict for National Public Radio.

p. 13 Several moments in this poem paraphrase John Milton's "On His
Blindness," and the concept of "the tyranny of the visual" comes from
Oliver Sacks's *The Mind's Eye* (New York: Knopf, 2010).

p. 17 The end of this poem paraphrases some of Olivier Messiaen's ideas
about prime numbers as they relate to rhythm.

p. 24 The last lines of this poem refer to Peter Shaffer's 1973 play,
Equus.

pp. 27–37 The death of the actor Andrew Grande is the subject of this
poem. This is the only poem in the collection that does not strictly
adhere to the prime-number principle. There are fourteen sections, to
echo the Stages of the Cross, and the fourteenth section has ninety-three
lines, for the Trinity.

pp. 36–37 The brief quote is my variation of a few well-known lines from
Dante's *Inferno*, Canto III.

p. 44 This poem creates its own version, from several other versions, of a story supposedly about the ancient poet Simonides, the father of mnemonics, or "memory theater."

p. 59 The poets in the first two stanzas are Dante Alighieri and Elmi Bodheri; Homer's *Iliad* is alluded to in the third.

pp. 61–62 The setting is the Lidice Museum and Memorial in the Czech Republic.

p. 63 General biographical information about the early Renaissance painter Giotto informs this poem.

p. 67 This poem was inspired by Enrique Metinides's photograph *Retrieval of a Drowned Person in Lake Xochimilco with the Public Reflected in the Water.*

p. 71 Cindy Sherman's "self portraits" are the basis for this poem.

p. 79 This poem is inspired by a series of paintings by Andrea Carlson that juxtapose figures from Native American mythology with pieces of Western art.

pp. 80–81 The subject matter for this poem comes from the ancient theologian Evagrius Ponticus's writings on *acedia* (translated variously as "despondency," "melancholia," "depression"), a sin that was thrown out because there seemed to be no remedy for it.

pp. 84–85 Eadweard Muybridge's and Thomas Eakins's various moving images and photographs from the nineteenth century inspired this poem.

p. 86 Frank Capra's *It's a Wonderful Life* is the movie referred to in this poem.

p. 87 Lennart Hjulström's *A Hill on the Dark Side of the Moon* is the film mentioned at the end of this poem.

p. 94 The starting point for this poem is Jean-Jacques Beineix's film, *Diva*.

p. 98 The end of the poem puts into first-person commentary a fifteenth-century chronicle by Alfonso de Palencia defaming Enrique IV of Castile. A solitary nature was considered evidence of deviance, homosexuality in particular. Palencia is quoted in Barbara F. Weissberger's *Isabel Rules: Constructing Queenship, Wielding Power* (Minneapolis: University of Minnesota Press, 2004).

p. 100 This poem is in response to Paul Klee's painting *Rose Wind*.

LITERATURE
is not the same thing as
PUBLISHING

Coffee House Press began as a small letterpress operation in 1972 and has grown into an internationally renowned nonprofit publisher of literary fiction, essay, poetry, and other work that doesn't fit neatly into genre categories.

Coffee House is both a publisher and an arts organization. Through our *Books in Action* program and publications, we've become interdisciplinary collaborators and incubators for new work and audience experiences. Our vision for the future is one where a publisher is a catalyst and connector.

Funder Acknowledgments

Coffee House Press is an internationally renowned independent book publisher and arts nonprofit based in Minneapolis, MN; through its literary publications and *Books in Action* program, Coffee House acts as a catalyst and connector—between authors and readers, ideas and resources, creativity and community, inspiration and action.

Coffee House Press books are made possible through the generous support of grants and donations from corporate giving programs, state and federal support, family foundations, and the many individuals who believe in the transformational power of literature. This activity is made possible by the voters of Minnesota through a Minnesota State Arts Board Operating Support grant, thanks to the legislative appropriation from the arts and cultural heritage fund and a grant from the Wells Fargo Foundation Minnesota. Coffee House also receives major operating support from the Amazon Literary Partnership, the Bush Foundation, the Jerome Foundation, the McKnight Foundation, Target, and the National Endowment for the Arts (NEA). To find out more about how NEA grants impact individuals and communities, visit www.arts.gov.

Coffee House Press receives additional support from the Alexander Family Foundation; the Archer Bondarenko Munificence Fund; the Elmer L. & Eleanor J. Andersen Foundation; the David & Mary Anderson Family Foundation; the Buuck Family Foundation; the Carolyn Foundation; the Dorsey & Whitney Foundation; Dorsey & Whitney LLP; the Knight Foundation; the Rehael Fund of the Minneapolis Foundation; the Matching Grant Program Fund of the Minneapolis Foundation; the Schwab Charitable Fund; Schwegman, Lundberg & Woessner, P.A.; the Scott Family Foundation; the US Bank Foundation; VSA Minnesota for the Metropolitan Regional Arts Council; the Archie D. & Bertha H. Walker Foundation; and the Woessner Freeman Family Foundation in honor of Allan Kornblum.

The Publisher's Circle of Coffee House Press

Publisher's Circle members make significant contributions to Coffee House Press's annual giving campaign. Understanding that a strong financial base is necessary for the press to meet the challenges and opportunities that arise each year, this group plays a crucial part in the success of Coffee House's mission.

Recent Publisher's Circle members include many anonymous donors, Mr. & Mrs. Rand L. Alexander, Suzanne Allen, Patricia A. Beithon, Bill Berkson & Connie Lewallen, the E. Thomas Binger & Rebecca Rand Fund of the Minneapolis Foundation, Robert & Gail Buuck, Claire Casey, Louise Copeland, Jane Dalrymple-Hollo, Jennifer Kwon Dobbs & Stefan Liess, Mary Ebert & Paul Stembler, Chris Fischbach & Katie Dublinski, Kaywin Feldman & Jim Lutz, Sally French, Jocelyn Hale & Glenn Miller, the Rehael Fund-Roger Hale/Nor Hall of the Minneapolis Foundation, Randy Hartten & Ron Lotz, Jeffrey Hom, Carl & Heidi Horsch, Amy L. Hubbard & Geoffrey J. Kehoe Fund, Kenneth Kahn & Susan Dicker, Stephen & Isabel Keating, Kenneth Koch Literary Estate, Jennifer Komar & Enrique Olivarez, Allan & Cinda Kornblum, Leslie Larson Maheras, Lenfestey Family Foundation, Sarah Lutman & Rob Rudolph, the Carol & Aaron Mack Charitable Fund of the Minneapolis Foundation, George & Olga Mack, Joshua Mack, Gillian McCain, Mary & Malcolm McDermid, Sjur Midness & Briar Andresen, Maureen Millea Smith & Daniel Smith, Peter Nelson & Jennifer Swenson, Marc Porter & James Hennessy, Jeffrey Scherer, Jeffrey Sugerman & Sarah Schultz, Nan G. & Stephen C. Swid, Patricia Tilton, Stu Wilson & Melissa Barker, Warren D. Woessner & Iris C. Freeman, Margaret Wurtele, Joanne Von Blon, and Wayne P. Zink.

For more information about the Publisher's Circle and other ways to support Coffee House Press books, authors, and activities, please visit www.coffeehousepress.org/support or contact us at info@coffeehousepress.org.

Greg Hewett Recommends

Cross Worlds
edited by Anne Waldman
and Laura Wright

The Falling Down Dance
by Chris Martin

Null Set
by Ted Mathys

The Open Curtain
by Brian Evenson

Prelude to Bruise
by Saeed Jones

GREG HEWETT is the author of *darkacre, The Eros Conspiracy, Red Suburb,* and *To Collect the Flesh*—poetry collections that have received a Publishing Triangle Award, two Minnesota Book Award nominations, a Lambda Literary Award nomination, and an Indie Bound Poetry Top Ten recommendation. His poetry has appeared in a variety of publications, including, most recently, the *Boston Review, Catamaran, Denver Quarterly, Disquieting Muses Quarterly,* and *Hanging Loose.* The recipient of Fulbright fellowships to Denmark and Norway, he has also been a fellow at the Camargo Foundation in France and is a professor of English at Carleton College.

Blindsight was designed by
Bookmobile Design & Digital Publisher Services.
Text is set in Ehrhardt MT Pro, a typeface designed
by Monotype Design Studio in 1991.